THE LITTLE BOOK OF
GREEN TIPS
A practical guide to a Green lifestyle

THE LITTLE BOOK OF
GREEN TIPS
A practical guide to a Green lifestyle

This edition first published in the UK in 2008
By Green Umbrella Publishing

© Green Umbrella Publishing 2008

www.gupublishing.co.uk

Publishers Jules Gammond & Vanessa Gardner

Printed and bound in China

ISBN 978-1-906229-62-7

THE LITTLE BOOK OF
GREEN TIPS
A practical guide to a Green lifestyle

Written by David Curnock

refused to

once called

re·cy·cle

that has

system of

1

Green living should not be confined to the lifestyle of the so-called 'eco-warriors': it must be the aim of each and every one of us to reduce our own impact on the environment. A few simple changes, when applied to our everyday activities both in the home and elsewhere, could have a relatively small impact on us as individuals but, cumulatively, will have an overall beneficial effect on the environment. We must all take responsibility for our own actions, while encouraging others to do likewise, and reduce the carbon footprint left behind as we go about our daily business. Don't wait for others to act first, take positive steps, every single day, to help safeguard the future of our planet. Carry out a review of your own lifestyle – and make some changes for the better, now!

2

Starting at home, some simple everyday changes in our behaviour patterns will help to improve the environment and, ultimately, benefit us all. Whether it be in terms of reducing waste, or improving our fitness and health, every little we can do towards saving natural resources will be worthwhile, and have a positive impact on the natural world. Knowledge of rocket science is not necessary; having accepted that we, as humans, are damaging our planet, it is obvious that we need to do something to prevent, or reduce, environmental calamity. Think before you act – it's not someone else's problem.

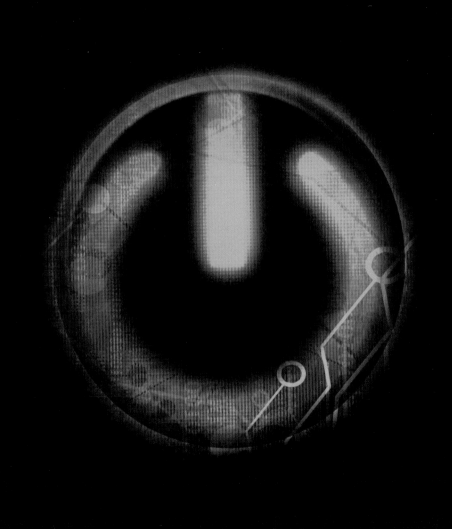

3

Find ways to economise on energy, throughout the home. Purchasing an energy meter will soon show where electrical power is being used and, perhaps, being wasted. This portable unit needs no wiring, and can be carried from room to room. It will show where power is being consumed, and where potential savings may be made. Energy meters are obtainable from eco-stores such as BritishEco, and could recoup the initial cost in the first year by helping to reduce wasteful energy consumption. Claims of savings of up to 25% on the cost of electricity bills, through a reduction in wastage, have been attributed to this item.

4

Always switch off electrical appliances when not in use. Many electrical items use power, even when not in use, unless they are properly switched off, so make sure the main power switch is turned to OFF, not left in 'standby' mode. Even on relatively low powered items, the standby system uses a significant amount of energy that adds to the quantity of carbon dioxide (CO_2) released into the atmosphere during power generation. Help to reduce the effect of greenhouse gases on the planet and, at the same time, reduce your energy bill; every penny wasted is a penny that could have been saved. Pennies add up to pounds.

5

Solar energy can be put to good use in providing for up to 70% of the daily hot water requirements of an average household. While solar hot water systems are not particularly cheap, they do play a part in greatly reducing CO_2 emissions, in fact, to zero!, over those given off from conventional water heating sources. A solar-powered system still produces some hot water when the sun is partially obscured by clouds, so it continues to operate, albeit on a somewhat reduced scale, during winter. Any southerly-facing roof is suitable and, once installed, the system is virtually maintenance free.

6

Some of the home's power requirements can be met by the installation of a solar domestic power station. In this system, a free-standing solar panel supplies DC electrical energy to a battery, from which the output is then converted, by an inverter, into AC electricity that can then be used to power some domestic appliances, ranging from TVs, lamps, and chargers. The amount of power available is dependant on the chosen size of solar panel, battery, and inverter, and can be backed up by power supplied from other renewable sources, such as wind power, in favourable conditions.

7

All those little LED indicator lamps on the front of your electrical equipment are fairly obvious reminders that the unit is either on, or in standby mode. What may be less apparent is the fact that charging adaptors for smaller, portable items such as mobile phones and media players often do not have a power indicator, or may be plugged in to a power socket that is not readily visible. These chargers contain an electrical transformer/rectifier that converts mains AC power to low-voltage DC power, and still uses power when not actually charging your accessories, so switch them off, or unplug from the mains, when not in use.

8

A useful accessory that may help to economise on all that unnecessary electrical usage is the remotely controlled power plug kit. This kit has several socket adaptors than can each carry a multiple-socket power block with a maximum total loading of 3,860W, and a hand-held remote control. This can be programmed to switch off all unnecessary power from up to four individual power sources, or from zones comprising several groups of socket adaptors. You can, effectively, be the master of your entire range of electrical equipment from the comfort of your armchair. You could also save yourself up to £40 each year!

9

Nothing is better than a nice cup of tea or a coffee break when at home. Save time, money, and the planet, by only boiling as much water as is needed for the purpose. Most modern kettles are either transparent, or fitted with a water level gauge, so it is worth measuring the required amount of water, using the intended cup or mug, into the kettle, and noting where the level comes up to on the gauge. Next time there will be no need to measure it out, and you will be having that nice drink much sooner than before.

10

Keep your fridge and freezer full, as this is the most energy-efficient way to run them. Bulk purchases of meat and produce, from your local supplier (of course!), will help towards this end. If you have to let your freezer run at less than full capacity, fill the otherwise empty space with loaves of bread, or place empty cardboard boxes inside, to reduce the volume that has to be cooled: this will save energy, as the motor will need to run much less in order to maintain the required temperature.

11

During the heating season, draw the curtains as soon as it gets dark; this prevents some of your heat from being lost to the outside. Better still, fit thermally-lined curtains, or hang separate thermal linings outside your normal fabric curtains. These can increase the thermal insulation by a significant amount and help to keep the rooms cosy without having to turn up the heating. In hot, sunny weather, keep the curtains closed in rooms that receive direct sunlight. Thermal linings will work in the reverse manner by helping to prevent the room from becoming too hot, thereby reducing the need for artificial cooling.

12

Turn off lighting when leaving a room unoccupied for more than a few minutes. Is that fancy mood lighting really necessary? The simple act of turning off all unnecessary lights can save pounds off your utility bill, so be conscious of the cost at all times. Lights left on for safety reasons, eg, for young children or the elderly to visit the bathroom, can be fitted with an inexpensive movement sensor that will switch on the light, automatically, when needed. A time delay unit will then switch the light off again, when it is no longer required.

13

Outside lighting for a porch, or alongside the footpath to your house, should be controlled by a movement sensor, and not left on throughout the night. Who is likely to visit at 2.00am? Alternatively, exterior and ornamental lighting for the garden, or front door welcome lights, can be solar powered. These attractively-designed lighting units are relatively inexpensive and can be placed almost anywhere, as they do not require any electrical wiring; once purchased, their running costs are zero. The garden fountain or water feature can also be solar powered, so switch off that mains-powered pump, and start to save money – no need for outdoor wiring and safety cut-out units, either.

14

Change to low-energy light bulbs. In the EU, legislation is expected that will make it illegal to sell ordinary light bulbs, following the lead set by Australia, where they will be banned in 2011. While it will not be illegal in the EU to continue to use ordinary bulbs, it is sensible to change to low-energy lighting as soon as possible. Low-energy light bulbs use less electrical energy – approximately 20-25% of that used by an equivalent regular tungsten bulb, hence, a reduction in both the running costs and the consequent CO_2 emissions. Fluorescent strip lighting also uses around 40% less energy that an equivalent tungsten light bulb.

15

Insulate your home! Save energy – and reduce your outgoings – by preventing unnecessary heat loss. UK government initiatives have made funding available, to many householders, that will help to offset the cost of insulating a home: in some cases, this is in the form of a grant (ie free!), so get something back from all those taxes you have paid, or have yet to pay, over the years. Government-sponsored schemes also include provisions for loft insulation, draught-proofing, hot water cylinder lagging, and low-energy light bulbs. Enquire at local council offices or Citizens Advice Bureau for details. Those of limited means may even receive funds towards the installation of an entire central heating system.

16

Reduce draughts wherever possible. Even a small gap between an external door, or single-glazed window, and its frame can cause a draught that will reduce the room temperature by a significant amount. If a gap of only 3mm around an external door is not sealed, it will provide an opening of similar area to that of a fully-open letterbox flap. Fit adequate draught proofing around the door frame – and don't forget that to draught-proof that letterbox, too! An unused, open fireplace will generate cold, in the form of draughts, so blank it off, but don't forget to allow some air to pass through, otherwise dampness in the chimney could become a problem.

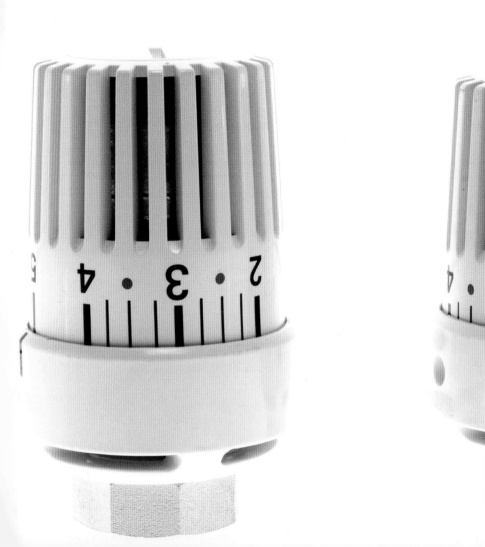

17

Place reflective foil behind radiators, particularly those fitted against the outside walls of your home. This is a relatively inexpensive precaution and will prevent some of the heat from being lost through the wall and, in conjunction with cavity wall insulation, will reduce your energy bills. Saving heat in this way will allow your individual radiator thermostats – you do have these fitted, don't you? – to be turned down with little, or no, noticeable effect on comfort. Reflective foil can be purchased from most DIY stores; a cheap alternative is to use cooking foil, although fixing it in place could be more problematic than when using the proprietary item.

18

Double glazing is another means of both saving energy, and reducing heating costs. The heat loss (U value) of a single pane window is 5.6. Double glazing with ordinary glass has a lower U value of 2.8. Double glazing with Pilkington K Glass TM has a U value of only 1.9, considerably better than conventional double glazing, and as good as triple glazing. All new double glazing units should be manufactured using specialist glass products such as Pilkington K TM, or Warm-a-Glass TM, the latter of which has an even lower U value of around 1.4 – one quarter of that of a single pane window.

19

If there are local shops, walk to them, rather than taking the car. Short journeys are particularly wasteful of fuel, and also the most polluting, as vehicle engines are less efficient over short distances. It is likely that you may even get to know your neighbours, as they walk to the shops with you! You will also be helping to prevent the decline of the smaller businesses in the area so, do yourself, and the local shopkeeper, a favour. Exercise and friendship costs nothing – using the car will cost the earth.

20

When leaving the house empty for that holiday or weekend away, switch off the central heating system entirely or, if there is a risk of freezing, leave it on its frost setting. Most heating systems have a programmable controller that allows heating 'on' and 'off' times to be set. Do you really need the heat on after the occupants have left for work or school? Check that heating times are set to complement your lifestyle, and reduce all of the 'time on' settings by at least 15 minutes, especially on those working days when you are rushing around prior to leaving the house.

21

Fix that dripping tap! On its own, a dripping tap could waste up to 90 litres of water in just one week, or over 4,600 litres in a year – all for the want of a simple tap washer. The water dripping from the tap will, almost certainly, leave an unsightly scale residue in the bath or wash basin, too. Think of water as a precious resource – it is! You wouldn't leave your full bottle of beer, wine, or soft drink lying on its side with the top undone, so don't leave the reservoir drain valve (your tap!) open.

22

Take a shower instead of having a bath. Apart from saving water, this can be a more refreshing exercise than the traditional method of bathing, especially if a cooler water temperature is selected. However, the saving does not apply when using a power shower: for the same length of time in use as for a regular shower, the power shower can actually use more water than filling a bath. It is worth bearing this in mind when choosing new bathroom equipment.

23

Reduce your water usage, by up to 70%, by installing spray taps in your kitchen and bathroom. Where it is not economically viable to change the taps themselves, many taps can be fitted with spray adaptors, for less than £5 per tap, which will help save this precious resource, and keep household bills in check. Shower heads can also be either replaced, or converted, using a low-flow adaptor; this adaptor can improve the feel of the shower as it produces a finer spray pattern. Most of the spray tap and shower adaptors can be fitted without the need for a plumber!

24

When doing the family laundry, use an eco-friendly washing powder or liquid. These products have a minimal effect on the environment and, for most types of laundry, will produce similar results to those of ordinary products. Use the washing machine on the coolest available washing cycle; 30ºC is suggested as giving the best results with most modern appliances. Newer washing machines have a short 'economy' programme that is both good for the clothes being washed, and have a less adverse impact on the environment – it will save money on your utility bill, too!

25

Do not leave the tap running when you brush your teeth. When brushing for the recommended 2 minutes, twice daily, the amount of water escaping from an open tap could be around 10-12 litres, per person. This is equivalent to around 3,650 litres or so in a year and, for a family of four, their combined total wastage of around 14,600 litres (3,208 gallons) would quarter-fill an Olympic-size swimming pool. At 2007 prices, a large water supplier in southern England charged £1.28 per unit (1,000 litres), therefore considerable savings could be made on metered water charges, rather than allowing the greater part of £19 to gurgle down the drain, each year!

26

Use environmentally-friendly products for cleaning tasks around the house. These products can be obtained from eco-stores, but there are often ready-made substitutes already close at hand. From the fruit basket, the lemon provides a versatile and effective substitute for bleach. Its natural qualities make it useful for removing stains on clothing, and for cleaning bathroom and kitchen surfaces. It helps to reduce lime scale, and is a safe disinfectant on chopping boards. Additionally, it comes with a fresh lemon fragrance, at no extra charge, so there is less need for perfumed aerosol products.

27

White vinegar is a cheap and efficient cleaning agent, and can be used to good effect on stainless steel sinks and cookware, leaving them bright and shiny. Windows and mirrors will sparkle after being cleaned with a water and vinegar mixture, as will other glass surfaces. A small amount of vinegar mixed with olive oil is a natural wood polish, if applied sparingly, then polished off with a soft, clean cloth. Test on a small area before attempting to polish that valuable antique table or cabinet; otherwise, use a natural product containing beeswax.

28

Baking soda, also known as bicarbonate of soda, when mixed with water, is a mild abrasive that is good for cleaning sinks, baths, and toilets, without damaging the surface. A stronger mixture can be used to degrease cookers, hobs, and splash-backs. A solution containing water, white vinegar, and bicarbonate of soda, is helpful when cleaning drains. For cleaning and deodorising refrigerators, a little baking soda on a damp cloth, when used to wipe all internal surfaces, is food-safe and effective. Remove stains from coffee, blood, sweat, and grass, with a solution of 1 part Borax, diluted with 8 parts of water.

29

Bare floorboards can be a design statement, or a money-saving answer to those flooring problems – but they may also be allowing draughts to ruin the cosy atmosphere, as well as adding to the heating bill! Seal gaps between floorboards using a sealing mastic or, with those old newspapers that you have kept under the stairs, instead of sending them for recycling. These can be made into papier-mâché, and the mixture forced into the gaps between boards. Do not block off ventilation bricks, or grills in rooms where there is a gas appliance – this could prove fatal!

30

Further savings can be made in the garden, with the provision of a water butt to collect rainwater from the roof guttering. Apart from any financial advantage, rain collected in water butts and other storage systems can provide a useful supply of water for the garden, especially in times of drought, when there may be a ban on the use of hosepipes and sprinklers. For the serious gardener, it may be worthwhile investing in a large capacity, underground water reservoir. This can provide sufficient rainwater storage to last throughout long periods of drought restrictions, to help keep plants healthy, and promote good cropping.

31

Where space and finance considerations allow, consider the installation of a domestic waste water recovery system. Water from baths, showers, and wash basins, is led into a storage tank that could provide a valuable source of water for use in the garden and around the house. Special filters allow water to be recycled for toilet flushing, laundry, vehicle washing, and many other uses. This, often almost clean, water would otherwise disappear down the drain, thereby wasting a precious resource. A little water can go a long way, saving you money and, at the same time, helping the environment.

32

The WC can use up to 9 litres of water per flushing. Although legislation now requires all WC cisterns to have water economy devices or a reduced amount of flush water, there are ways to improve water economy without changing your bathroom units. The classic water-saving device, namely a brick placed in the cistern, has been replicated in a more elegant manner with the introduction of a polythene container that fits inside the cistern. This retains around 33% of the water that would otherwise be flushed, and recovers its cost within around 12 weeks, in the average family bathroom.

33

If spending money is against your natural instincts, instead, try resetting the level at which the float valve shuts off the water supply. This straightforward procedure can be carried out by anybody who is reasonably competent at DIY, but remember to check that the amount of water flushed is sufficient to do the job properly; failure to do so would result in even greater water wastage if there is a need for repeated flushing. Also, consider whether flushing is necessary after every visit – the decision is yours!

34

Where possible, dry your laundry in the open air. This offers multiple advantages over the tumble-drier or combined washer-drier. Apart from the more obvious environmental and financial benefits, the laundry will, where this is necessary, be easier to iron, giving further savings. It will also smell fresher, thereby reducing the need for artificial fresheners. You will also benefit from the fresh air and light exercise involved when putting out, or taking in, the washing. Where a drier is the only solution, always use the shortest cycle, make sure that the drier filter is kept clean, and empty the evaporator tank, if fitted, before use.

35

Keep track of your utility bills: consider changing to a supplier that generates electricity from renewable, or sustainable sources. Some utility suppliers have special 'green' tariffs that give consumers the choice of donating a small portion of their bill towards an eco-friendly project overseas; this will benefit those developing countries by allowing them to choose a less climate-damaging source of power, particularly in areas where there is no existing power infrastructure. Every little helps, so it is worthwhile considering this option.

36

Think about recycling. Most local authorities have developed both domestic and commercial recycling facilities – use them. Apart from the obvious benefit to the environment, recycling helps to reduce the cost of waste collection, and reduces the amount of waste going to landfill – a resource that is, itself, rapidly disappearing (no pun intended). Try to find an alternative method of disposal for items that are still serviceable, but no longer required. Furniture, clothing, soft furnishings, and the like, can be passed on to charitable bodies who redirect them to the needy. This will help to improve the lives of the less fortunate and, at the same time, extend the useful life of the item.

TIPS 37 & 38

37

What about those old daily and Sunday papers? These can be sent for recycling, of course, but you can also use them to provide heat for the home, where this is by means of a solid-fuel fire or stove. With a log maker, these newspapers can be compressed and transformed into a useful and cost-efficient fuel, as the logs can each burn for up to one hour. Log makers, and many other eco-friendly and fair-trade products for the home and the workplace, are available from sources such as Natural Collection, Recycled Products Online, and many others.

38

Is there an imminent wedding in your family or circle of friends? It is not widely known that one wedding day adds at least 14.5 tonnes of CO_2 to the atmosphere, so do your bit to help redress the balance by offsetting some of the damage. Suggest to the happy couple that their wedding gift list should include only those items made from recycled or sustainable resources, or that gift vouchers, from an eco-store, be purchased. For the couple that has everything, how about an 'ethical' gift? This could be in the form of money donated to an organisation, such as Oxfam Unwrapped, which provides books, goats or even beehives, to benefit those communities in developing countries.

THE LITTLE BOOK OF GREEN TIPS | 45

39

Cut back on unnecessary paperwork, both at work and at home. Households with access to an internet connection can arrange for paperless billing for most services provided by banks, utility suppliers, motoring services, and a whole range of on-line shops and service providers. Airline reservations can be booked on-line, and the booking reference sent to the traveller by SMS text on their mobile phone, thus removing the need for paper. Financial investments, stocks and shares, and the like, can be checked over the internet, either at home or at your bank or investment broker.

40

So – you are fed up with all that junk mail that pours through the letterbox almost every day, right? Direct mail marketing has more than doubled in the UK since 1990. Most of it goes, unopened, straight into the bin – make sure it is recycled! Not all direct mail is bad – but you, not the direct mail company, should be the one to choose whether you wish to receive it! Register your wish not to receive such mail with the UK Mailing Preference Service (internet URL at the end of this book). Help to reduce waste.

41

Beware of the unnecessary print-out! Do you really need a hard copy? Some things can be printed, for a personal record, on paper that has previously been used. Provided that the paper is not creased, and therefore likely to jam the printer, try reloading it, and print on the other side. The old adage 'save paper – save money', while still being true, could easily apply to the environmental consideration, also. Use the reverse of single-sided, printed matter as scribble pads for the children, for note-taking at work (bearing in mind the need for confidentiality of any sensitive printed matter), and notes for the milkman, etc.

42

If you are reasonably fit, why not go for a brisk walk or cycle ride? Healthy exercise is good for the body and the mind, and will present an opportunity to commune with nature. In colder weather, exercise will not only do you some good, it will also, subject to the correct clothing being worn, raise your body temperature so that when you return home, there will be less need to turn up the heating. You will already have saved on the heating while you were taking exercise because you turned the heating down or, better still – OFF, before you went out, didn't you?

43

Many people commute over many miles, each day, simply to get to their place of work. With the advent of modern electronic communications systems, workers could save hours that are wasted on commuting, and reduce the pollution generated on their individual journeys by car, motorcycle, and even public transport, if they worked from home. Radical-thinking companies make provision for some of their staff to work from home, using company intranet, the internet, and other forms of communication. If you work in an occupation that lends itself to this home working, then ask your employer if this is possible. He could also benefit from need for less office space to be bought or rented, too!

44

If commuting is unavoidable, try and work out the best means of travel, both in terms of the carbon dioxide and other pollutants emitted from the vehicle, as well as the cost involved. An average car produces around 10.4kg of CO_2 for each gallon of petrol consumed, or 1kg in every 3.75 miles (6km) assuming a fuel consumption of 39mpg: travelling by bus or train produces 1kg per person for each 6.5 miles travelled. These figures speak for themselves: walking and cycling both produce extremely small amounts of CO_2 by comparison.

45

Where possible, take advantage of flexi-time working hours to travel to and from work outside the main rush hour. With ever changing modern lifestyles, there has been a trend towards less rigid work times as employers become more aware of the need for flexibility in working arrangements, to either recruit or retain their workforce. Workers can often reduce their commute time by travelling just a few minutes earlier or later than they would have to if working a rigid 9 to 5 day. Avoiding the rush hour would benefit the environment as well as the pocket, as less fuel would be used, leading to lower CO_2 emissions.

46

At work, make sure that all electrical equipment is switched off, when not being used. Computers should be switched off, or set to a power-saving mode, when unattended for more than a few minutes. This also applies to lighting: many offices and other workplaces do not have an energy-saving strategy in place. Do your bit, and either ask your employer to implement a scheme, or encourage your work colleagues to adopt an energy-conscious approach in their workplace. Switch lights off when the room is unoccupied!

47

That laptop is a useful item, but please don't leave it switched on when not required for use. Even when it is in hibernation mode, it can still consume up to 40W of power. So what if it is not connected to the mains supply? – does it really matter? Well, that laptop battery will have to be charged, sooner or later, so do think 'green' and do not leave it on, unless you are going to use it: better still, charge it with an eco-friendly charger, such as a clockwork, or solar powered, device.

48

Printer and photocopier cartridges should be recycled and not sent to landfill. Most companies will have a centralised print facility but, where this does not apply, there is the likelihood that many cartridges are replaced each year. Cartridges can usually be refilled using a simple kit, or returned to a depot or retail outlet for refilling. Encourage the use of these facilities, and remind users to print only when there is a specific need, rather than take a hard copy 'just in case'. The photocopier is an often abused, or misused, piece of office equipment; keep its use to a minimum, and make sure it is switched off when not required.

49

Where large amounts of paper waste are unavoidably generated, why not donate these to a nursery or school, so that they can be used for painting on, or in other art projects. Charities such as Children's Scrapstore will collect unwanted bulk items, free of charge, and will ensure that they are recycled by member groups. This charity also collects other items of safe waste from business which can re-used as a low cost, creative resource. As well as paper and card, they can accept foam, plastic pots, cardboard tubes and tubs, netting, fabric, books, CDs and all manner of offcuts and leftovers from business.

50

It may well be true that the hot drinks vending machine is the simple solution to staff refreshments in the office – but how 'green' is it? How much electrical power does it use? Is it switched off at night or over weekends? Are the cups provided by the vendor made from recycled (or recyclable) materials – and how are they disposed of? Where drinks are made with traditional kettles or coffee pots, use proper ceramic cups or mugs, rather than paper or polystyrene – and wash the cups afterwards, using an eco-friendly washing-up product, please!

51

Having ensured that all unnecessary office or factory lighting is switched off at night and at weekends, is there something else you may have forgotten? Make it the specific responsibility of you – the boss – or a member of staff, to check that no taps are left running in wash-rooms and galley areas. If auto-flushing systems have been installed in the urinals, do these flush throughout the night, weekends, or during works shut-downs for holidays? Manual press-button flushes, or proximity sensors can do the same job – automatic shut-off taps on washbasins are also a good idea, too!

52

Mobile phones have become more commonplace in recent times: they have also become something of a fashion accessory, as each new version offers more advanced technology along with the latest styling. Some mobile phone suppliers will take your older model in part exchange for a newer version. If this option is not available, don't just throw it away, give it to a charitable organisation who will ensure that it is either reused, for the benefit of others, or properly recycled, and thus prevent yet another potentially hazardous item from disappearing into a hole in the ground.

53

Avoid using disposable batteries in your portable electrical equipment; instead use rechargeable batteries. In some cases, the rechargeable items and their mains-powered charger will cost more than the disposable variety. The additional cost will soon be recouped, as the life of the rechargeable battery can be up to 40 times longer than the throwaway, thereby reducing lifetime cost and, as batteries are often used in twos or fours, saves many from ending up as landfill. After the first few recharges, you are in profit: the environmental impact will, from now onwards, be greatly reduced.

54

Alternatively, there is a product available that will recharge ordinary alkaline batteries. The product is generically known as a Battery Regenerator. Best results are obtained with premium grades of battery, eg, Duracell Plus, or similar. The regenerator will recharge the battery to 60-95% of its original capacity, and is totally safe in use. It is claimed that an alkaline battery can be regenerated up to between 60 and 100 times, depending on the type and condition. Cost of each charge is around ⅒th of a penny, although the process can take up to 72 hours, from a unit initially costing around £20.

55

For many small electrical gadgets, there is another option. Some years ago, an inventor, Trevor Baylis, revolutionised the lives of people in underdeveloped countries with his wind-up portable radio. This brought news, education and entertainment to those in remote areas where there was no mains electrical power; neither were there any corner shops that sold batteries! The clockwork-powered generator has since been refined, and is now available in many different guises and applications, such as a torch, a charger for mobile phones, and a personal media player. A few turns on a winding handle will power the torch for an hour or so, and all for around £20! (batteries not included – it doesn't need any).

56

Cyclists who would like to do that little bit extra for the environment, can also benefit from the wind-up torch concept as the same principle has been applied to both front and rear cycle lamps, including the popular LED style; there is no need to get caught out with a flat battery, ever again. Similarly, a lantern is available for emergency lighting, in the event of power failure in the home or, as a useful aid at the roadside in the event of a vehicle breakdown. Suppliers of these items can be found listed at the end of this book.

57

Solar power is one of the best known forms of sustainable energy. Less widely known is the fact that many products based on the solar principle are available for both home use, and as a source of power for portable items such as radios and other small gadgets, and mobile phone charging. There is even a range of solar chargers for batteries, thus providing a versatile, and valuable, energy-saving power supply. Solar power is also free, so it makes sense to use it, whenever possible. For a comparatively small initial outlay, most portable power requirements can be provided in an environmentally-friendly manner, and without incurring ongoing running costs.

58

For indoor situations where solar power is not an option, there are gadgets that are powered by water alone. Digital clocks, calculators, and desk novelties, are driven by a water cell that provides low voltage electrical power. The water cell contains two electrodes made from specially formulated alloys, one positive, the other negative. As soon as water comes in contact with both electrodes, an electrochemical reaction takes place, resulting in the production of electrical energy. To maintain a constant supply of energy, simply refill as the water evaporates. This water cell has a continuous life of at least 2 years.

59

Think about alternatives to the, so-called, school run. Thousands of unnecessary journeys are made by car, even though there is an alternative means of travel. Many schoolchildren attend a school that is less than a mile from their home, yet are driven to, and from, school on a daily basis. Without compromising safety, there are methods of travel that are greener alternatives, such as the walking bus, where several children actually walk to school together, supervised by volunteer parents who take turns on a rota basis. This method has the added benefit of giving the children – and their parents – regular exercise.

60

Where the school run is unavoidable, create a car pool arrangement with other parents in the area, similar to those used by some commuters. This could even be combined with after school activities to enhance the community spirit, as well as potentially reducing the number of vehicles around schools, an important safety consideration. Children who are proficient cyclists should be encouraged to cycle to school, where feasible, with road safety, and distance travelled, being taken into account. Otherwise, use public transport wherever possible.

61

Switch off your car engine when stationary. Apart from short pauses in progress due to traffic lights, etc, any delay in progress of other than a few seconds can result in the generation of unnecessary pollution, as well as adding to the cost of the journey. When it becomes obvious that there is a traffic problem other than a red traffic light, or stop / go board, switch off your engine. Some traffic jams last for hours. Where possible, plan your route to avoid known 'choke' points on the journey, and avoid travelling during peak periods.

62

In cold weather, take note of the weather forecast and cover the windscreen, and other windows of your vehicle, if it is left outside. This will reduce the need for chemical de-icing products, or the lengthy delay caused by having to scrape the windscreen on a cold morning. Do not leave the engine running longer than necessary: de-icing the outside of the windscreen by using the demister and fan on the inside is grossly inefficient, and does considerable damage to both the environment and your fuel bill. It doesn't do your engine and electrical system much good, either. Cover it up or, better still, put it in the garage instead, if you have one.

63

Drive off as soon as your vision is clear. Most modern vehicles have screen demisters that should keep the windows clear under most weather conditions. Learn how to operate the heating, demisting and air conditioning system – many people fail to read the vehicle handbook, and are not aware of the proper method of operation of these basic safety – and comfort – systems. If you have to keep stopping to clear the windows, you will not get the best economy from your vehicle and you will cause additional CO_2 to be discharged, while stationary.

64

Avoid revving the engine unnecessarily. Modern engines are designed to be driven immediately after starting; it is not necessary to let them warm up first. Revving the engine will not help the defroster or demister to work faster – it simply uses more fuel! If the windscreen is badly misted, wipe it with a demister cloth or damp chamois leather, not the back of your hand, before driving off. Special demisting cloths or fluids are best applied to a dry screen before it gets heavily misted: take a few minutes on a fine Sunday morning to clean all windows, not forgetting the inside.

65

In all climatic conditions it is essential to keep your vehicle running at its optimum performance level. Regular maintenance of the vehicle will ensure that its complex emission control system is working correctly, and any malfunction quickly detected and rectified. Apart from excessive smoke from the tailpipe due to burning oil, or an over-rich fuel/air mixture, the majority of combustion products are not visible. An emissions check forms an integral part of the mandatory MOT requirements for all vehicles over three years old.

66

Keep an eye on those tyre pressures. Apart from the obvious safety aspects, under-inflated tyres are illegal, will have an adverse effect on fuel economy, and could put penalty points on your driving licence. Lower tyre pressures increase the rolling resistance of the vehicle, and it will consume around 3% more fuel over a given distance than the same vehicle with correctly inflated tyres. Always ensure that the tyres are at the manufacturer's recommended value for the number of vehicle occupants and their luggage. Check the pressures are as recommended in the handbook, or on a diagram usually found inside or near the driver's door.

67

Would you like to save up to 15% on your motoring fuel costs? Installation of a Magno car fuel magnet is a simple DIY task and will soon recover its initial cost. This device basically consists of two magnets in a housing that is fitted around the fuel feed pipe and secured with cable ties. The magnets induce the formation of additional oxygen molecules between the fuel hydrocarbon molecules, thus improving combustion; this increases power, lowers fuel consumption, and reduces harmful emissions. The Magno device is claimed to be suitable for both petrol and diesel engines.

68

When replacing your vehicle, it is always a good idea to check the fuel economy rating of the vehicle under consideration. Personal car travel produces 13% of the UK's total greenhouse gas emissions, as well having a major impact on local air pollution. Since 2002, all new vehicles are allocated an official government fuel economy rating that takes into account both the fuel economy and emissions of the vehicle. The rating is then reflected in the vehicle tax band which favours the more fuel efficient, and therefore the least polluting, vehicles and results in lower vehicle tax payments by their owners.

EXPIRES EXPIRES EXPIRES 19

31 05 06

04CZK/P £115.00

DI

12

ALLER PARADE WESTON·S·MARE
W
24 Mi 05
Post Offic

DC

69

Even vehicles of a similar make and model can have significant variations in their tax banding, so it is worth studying a range of vehicles before making a decision. Some of the larger vehicles have a more fuel efficient sibling in the range. A typical 3-litre petrol-engined car will generally be in a higher tax band than its smaller-engined brother. Many small, modern diesel-powered vehicles are actually less polluting than their equivalent petrol-engined model, but can have a higher initial cost.

70

Not all can afford the luxury of a new car, but those fortunate enough to be able to choose one should consider the purchase of a fuel efficient and low-polluting vehicle. Hybrids and biofuel cars are becoming increasingly available, so the choice is yours. Data on fuel efficiency and emissions is readily available: all new cars for sale must be displayed with a label showing their economy rating. Further information can be found at the website of the Vehicle Certification Agency (URL given at the end of this book).

71

Biofuels are derived from sustainable resources and up to 5% biofuel is added during the production process for both petrol and diesel fuels. Some cars are available that can run on a blend of 85% bioethanol, known as E85: a UK government edict requires transport fuel suppliers to provide 5% of all fuel as biofuel, by 2011. Cars powered by fuel containing these natural sources of energy will also benefit from the lower vehicle tax bands.

72

For those expecting biofuelled cars to be slower than those more conventionally-fuelled, this concept has proved demonstrably incorrect. Announced in 2006, the Saab 9-5 Aero SportCombi, with a 2.3 litre turbocharged engine powered by bioethanol, produces almost 20% more maximum power, and 25% more torque, than its petrol fuelled equivalent. Its 0-60 acceleration time, should this be considered ethical, is around 6 seconds, as opposed to 6.9 seconds for the petrol-powered car. In Sweden, the E85 fuelled version accounts for more than 70% of total sales for the 9-5 model.

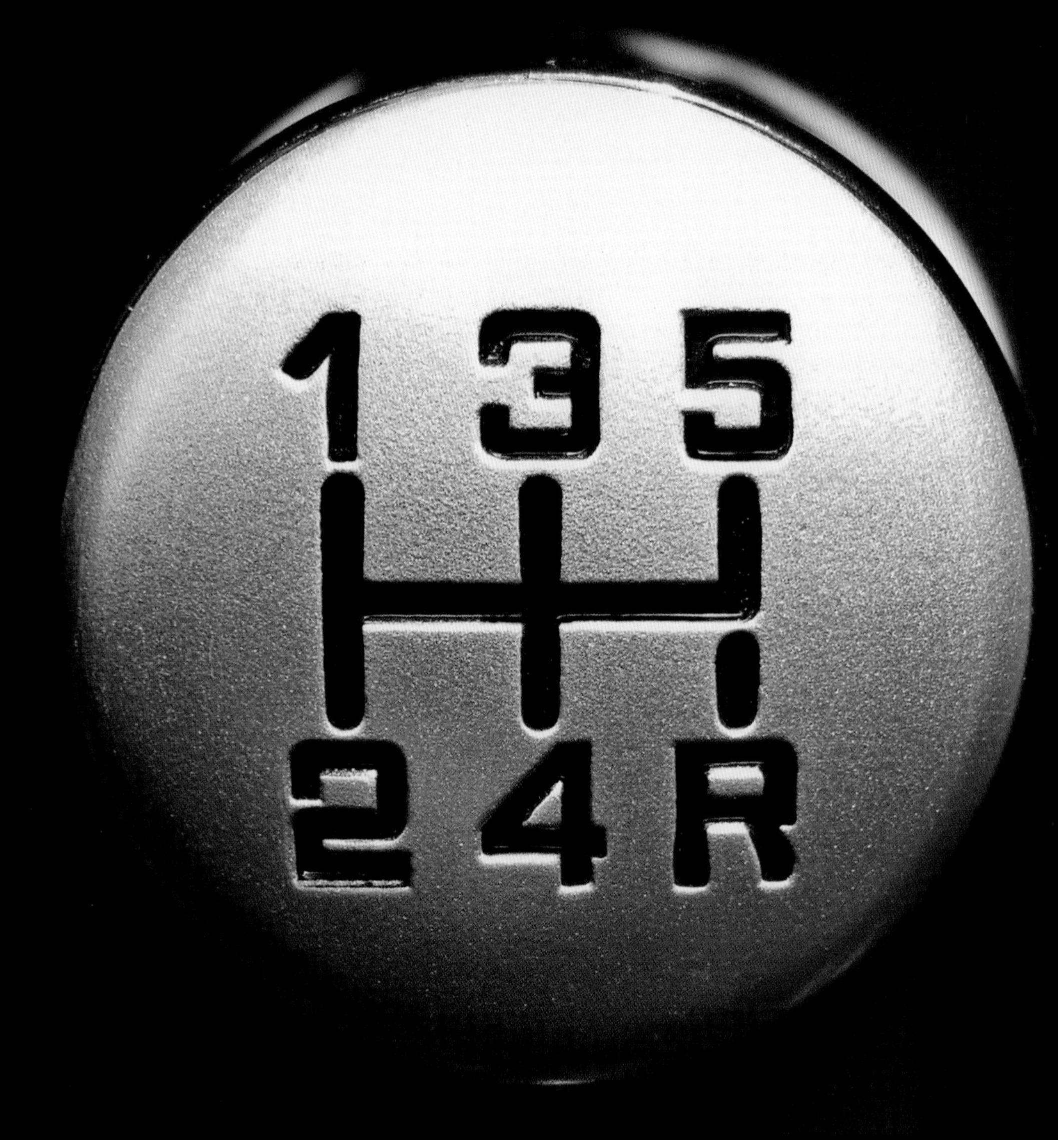
1 3 5
2 4 R

73

It's not only what you drive, but how you drive it, that can have a significant effect on fuel consumption, and therefore, emissions. Drive as smoothly as possible and check the road ahead for possible changes in traffic speed – avoid harsh braking and acceleration. As well as saving fuel, a smoother driving technique will result in both a less stressful journey, thereby adding to road safety, and greater consideration for other road users. Anticipate traffic light signals and slow gently when these are against you, they won't change any quicker if you brake hard from high speed.

74

Change up to a higher gear at the right time, rather than stay in a low gear that uses more revs. As a general rule, changing up at 2500rpm, for most petrol, and 2000rpm for diesel, cars will give the best results. A vehicle travelling at 37mph in third gear will use 25% more fuel than it would at the same speed in fifth gear. Also remember that, at 70mph, you could be using up to 30% more fuel than at 50mph. Road conditions and speed limits permitting, most vehicles will cruise most economically at around 56mph in top gear.

75

Unless they are actually being used, remove roof racks, top boxes, and caravan wind deflectors, before driving. On their own, these add weight to the vehicle, create additional wind resistance while increasing the noise level for the occupants, as well as ruining fuel economy. Similarly, the use of air conditioning, heater and interior cooling fans, and other electrical accessories can also affect economy. However, a properly programmed satellite navigation system can save money, by offering the choice of the most direct, or most economical, routeing, and some models give warning of traffic jams and other road problems.

76

When washing the car, use the time honoured 'bucket and sponge' method, rather than a hosepipe. The hose will use, on average, 7 or 8 times more water than when using a bucket. For those with an aversion to using the sponge, an accessory is available that has a wash brush and hose fed from a bucket; this supplies water to the brush through a valve system, activated by the brush movement, thereby reducing waste. This system is best used in conjunction with water from the garden water butt; this is generally softer than tap water, and less likely to cause spotting on the paintwork.

77

For those commuting to and from work by car, the car-pool system is a good way to save both money, and the environment. Car sharing offers not only environmental and cost-saving benefits, but can also reduce the overall journey time, with less vehicles being on the road. It can also provide companionship, instead of that lonely, repetitive journey, an important safety consideration on longer journeys. When you get to work, the chances of finding a parking space will be improved, as some of the erstwhile competition will be travelling with you!

78

When parking in multi-storey or supermarket car park, drive nose-in to the parking bay. Reverse parking is wasteful of fuel, for both you, and for other motorists who have to wait while you finish parking: it also generates unnecessary localised pollution. It is quicker and easier to park nose-in, and much easier to reverse out of the space, thus minimising the chance of parking scrapes. At planning consultations for new parking developments, you have an opportunity to enter objections to the development – insist on 'herring-bone' style parking layouts, as these discourage reverse parking, are inherently safer, aid traffic flow, and minimise waste and pollution.

79

Buy locally produced goods, wherever possible. Any item of fresh food that is not in season, or is not native to the UK, has probably clocked up many 'food miles' on its way to the shelf. Supermarkets and chain stores often source their products from overseas, even where these items are available at home; if these imported goods were ignored by shoppers, this would hit the profits of the national and multi-national companies involved. Local produce will probably have less packaging, too. Growers have, in recent years, adapted to the internet age, and offer locally-grown produce for home delivery.

80

Everybody is entitled to a holiday, finance and family circumstances permitting. Plan your holiday with the environmental impact in mind. Do you really need to fly long-haul when the same sun can be found on a beach, or in the countryside, much closer to home? Shorter travelling times mean that you will get there, and home again afterwards, much sooner, and thus extend the time available for the holiday itself. Do you have to travel on the first day of the school holidays? Roads, railways and airports are much busier at this time – why add to the 'sheer volume of traffic' – choose an alternative.

PAPER & CARDBOARD RECYCLING ONLY

81

When travelling by air is the only practical means, book your flights with an airline that demonstrates a greener attitude towards flying. Look for those with newer, more fuel-efficient fleets; choose a direct flight rather than one involving stopovers or indirect routings; offset your journey by signing up to a 'carbon offsetting' scheme that will be used to help compensate for the environmental damage caused by your travel. Such schemes are also available for those who, on a voluntary basis, recognise the need to atone for the fact that they have enlarged their own carbon footprint, whatever the means of travel.

82

Recycle as much household 'waste' as possible – excess or unwanted household products are only 'wasted' if they can be put to no further use, and end up as landfill. Segregate all items for recycling, and do your bit towards ensuring that domestic waste sent for landfill is kept to a minimum. It may be that, in the not too distant future, every household could be charged according to the amount of non-recyclable waste it produces, so it is a good idea to recycle as much as possible, starting from now!

USEFUL SOURCES OF INFORMATION

Advice on greener living:
www.direct.gov.uk/en/Environmentandgreenerliving

Suppliers of eco-gadgets:
www.ethicalsuperstore.com/products/trevor-baylis-brands
www.ecogadgets.co.uk

Vehicle fuel and emissions data:
www.vcacarfueldata.org.uk

Mailing Preference Service (UK):
www.mpsonline.org.uk/mpsr
Mailing Preference Service (MPS)
DMA House
70 Margaret Street
London
W1W 8SS
Complaints Department: Tel: 020 7291 3321

Fair trade and eco-friendly personal and domestic products:
www.naturalcollection.com
or by mail order from:
Natural Collection,
Dept 7306,
Sunderland SR9 9XZ

Writing instruments and stationery supplies:
www.recycledproductsonline.co.uk

Oxfam Unwrapped:
www.oxfamunwrapped.com

Rainwater harvesting systems and other environmentally friendly products:
www.britisheco.com

Water-saving spray taps and adaptors:
www.biggreenswitch.co.uk/around_the_home

Waste items from businesses for creative projects:
www.childrensscrapstore.co.uk
Branches throughout the UK (see your local business or telephone directory)

Carbon offset schemes:
www.co2balance.uk.com Tel: 0845 094 2620
www.carbonneutral.com/shop/index.asp
www.climatecare.org

Also available:

Available from all major stockists

The pictures in this book were provided courtesy of

GETTY IMAGES
www.gettyimages.com

SHUTTERSTOCK IMAGES
www.shutterstock.com

Design and artwork by David Wildish

Image research by Ellie Charleston

Creative Director: Kevin Gardner

Published by Green Umbrella Publishing

Publishers: Jules Gammond, Vanessa Gardner

Written by David Curnock